Digital Detox

Building Healthy Technology Habits for a More Present Life

Pauline Diane Edwards

Table of Contents

Almost everything will work again if you unplug
it for a few minutes, including you.

— Anne Lamott

Chapter 1. Introduction

In an increasingly digital world, the art of unplugging grows more essential by the day - but also more elusive. Stepping into the invigorating realm of "Digital Detox: Building Healthy Technology Habits for a More Present Life", this Special Report gets to the heart of creating a balance between our screen time and our 'me' time. Not too technical, rather personal and hands-on, this report is filled with actionable insights designed to catalyse a new depth of connection with ourselves and the world around us. Indicators highlight the damages of excessive screen time, effective strategies to curb digital dependence, and step-by-step guides to form healthier technology habits. So, take a break from your numerous screens, sit back, and dive headfirst into this transformative journey, offering you much-needed relief from the digital world and a blueprint to a more present, fulfilled life. Get ready to revolutionize your relationship with technology and make it a tool for enhancing your life, not draining it!

Chapter 2. Understanding Our Digital World: The Implications of Overuse

The proliferation of digital technology has enabled us to transcend societal norms, overcome geographical barriers, and innovate at an unprecedented rate. This technological advancement, however, comes with a distinct set of challenges. It is imperative to consider the impact this extraordinary reliance on technology poses to our individual existence and collective well-being. Are we harnessing technology, or is it subtly taking control over us? This chapter aims to elucidate these multifaceted prospects of our digital world.

2.1. The Digital Landscape: Here and Now

Our world is growing increasingly digital. Whether we're shopping online, making video calls, or collaborating on projects without physical barriers, our lives seem to revolve around the digital sphere. It's a real-time, global network that has transformed our experiences and perceptions of the world, and its potential is limitless. Nevertheless, a significant share of these interactions also predisposes us to tendencies of over-reliance and overuse.

Profoundly immersed in this digital culture, we've nearly forgotten the pre-digital era, when interactions were straightforward, personal, and less pervasive. The repercussions of this digital transformation, still unfolding, are increasingly affecting our lives, challenging our cognitive abilities, relationships, and overall wellness.

2.2. From Digital Convenience to Digital Addiction

Define digital addiction simply as an excessive attachment to our digital devices, making it challenging to disconnect even when not necessary. Or in some instances, it may manifest when our desire to stay online overpowers our need to attend to critical facets of our lives such as work, sleep, or personal interactions.

The boundary separating productive use of digital technology from possible overindulgence seems hazy and easily crossed. The addictive nature can be attributed to the immediate gratification it offers. The 'like' on social media, or an affirming email, provides instant dopamine hits, fostering a desire for more.

2.3. The Damages of Overusing Digital Devices

Overuse of digital technology can spiral into a myriad of issues. For instance, prolonged hours of screen time may lead to health problems such as fatigue, insomnia, or even more severe conditions such as obesity or heart diseases due to a sedentary lifestyle. Simultaneously, cognitive implications, encompassing reduced attention span or memory loss, are also symptomatic of excessive screen time.

The effects permeate beyond the individual level, on an interpersonal scale, excessive digital consumption may bring about disconnection or estrangement in relationships. The prevalence of digital dialogues seems to be undermining real-life interactions, causing what Sherry Turkle calls 'alone together' scenarios.

Learning to harness this unprecedented level of digital integration into our lives means recognizing our vulnerabilities to the digital world's more insidious aspects. As we proceed in this journey, clearly delineating between healthy use and overuse becomes indispensable.

2.4. Navigating the Digital Age

Humankind's story is one of adaptation. And navigating this digital age calls for precisely this quality. If we aim to leverage the numerous advantages technology provides us, we must also learn to balance it with well-founded self-awareness and control.

Mindfulness towards our digital habits is the first step in recognizing overuse and taking measures to prevent it. Formulating a symbiotic relationship with technology, instead of a parasitic one, lets us truly exploit the potential that this digital revolution promises.

Holistically, the message isn't to reject technology, but rather, to harness it efficiently and mindfully. In the following chapters, we'll further explore this domain, delving into the specific psychological, physical, and emotional costs of digital overuse. We will also address how to build a more balanced digital lifestyle, replete with beneficial technology habits.

Chapter 3. The Mental Minor: How Digital Overload Affects Your Brain

In the contemporary information age, we must acknowledge the increasing complexity of our relationship with technology, particularly our pervasive handheld devices. These devices have become a lifeline for many, a trusted confidante and assistant. However, in the vast spectrum of our digital involvement, a darker side lurks. This chapter aspires to shed light on the intricate web of mental effects brought on by our increased and often hyperactive engagement with these digital tools, focusing on the critical role of the brain as a processing hub in dealing with digital overload.

3.1. Understanding Digital Overload

Firstly, it is crucial to grasp the meaning of the term 'digital overload'. Essentially, this phrase denotes an intense inundation of digital content, be it through emails, messages, newsfeeds, or any number of online sources. This information deluge often results in feelings of stress, anxiety, and a sense of being overwhelmed. In our quest to remain connected and informed, we unconsciously allow our brains to be overburdened by an avalanche of information flowing from our screens.

This state of chronic multitasking might give one a facade of productivity, however the underlying impact on the brain is far from beneficial. Consider this, when we are constantly switching between tasks or being incessantly interrupted by notifications, our mental resources are scattered, resulting in diminished focus, impaired memory, and a reduced ability to make decisions.

3.2. Cognitive Consequences of Digital Overload

The brain is a marvel of biological engineering, capable of processing vast amounts of information. Nonetheless, like any intricate machinery, it has limitations. In the face of digital overload, various cognitive abilities can suffer.

A relentless barrage of digital information fragments our attention, leading to a phenomenon known as 'Continuous Partial Attention'. In this state, we remain partially attentive to multiple sources of information without fully concentrating on any. This divided attention can lead to weakened memory consolidation, reduced comprehension and overall cognitive exhaustion.

Moreover, their incessant demands for interaction, digital devices encourage a state of hyper-alertness that results in mental fatigue. Prolonged periods of this constant mental engagement can potentially lead to burnout, chronic stress, or anxiety disorders.

In fact, researchers have noted a new condition emerging in recent years - Digital Amnesia, also known as 'the Google effect'. This occurs when we subconsciously forget information that can be easily found online, suggesting a significant shift in our memory patterns due to digital technology.

3.3. Neuroplasticity and Digital Technology

Our brains are not static. They change and adapt in response to our experiences, a characteristic known as neuroplasticity. This adaptability is generally beneficial, but it can also lead to less favorable alterations when it comes to our interaction with digital technology.

Due to the fast-paced, instant-gratification nature of the digital world, our brains are rewiring to adapt to this rapid speed of information acquisition, creating neural pathways that favor short-term, fleeting attention. This has led researchers to speculate about possible long-term impacts on deep-thinking abilities, creativity, and problem-solving skills, which rely on sustained and focused attention.

Years of conditioning through the 'scroll and swipe' culture may also impact our patience, lowering our tolerance for slower-paced activities and fostering a need for constant stimulation.

3.4. Digital Overload and Mental Health

Excessive digital consumption contributes to mental health issues such as anxiety and depression. The continuous exposure to others' lives through social media platforms can foster a sense of comparison and inadequacy, heightening feelings of self-doubt and lowering self-esteem. Simultaneously, the compulsive need to check and interact with digital devices can lead to addiction-like behaviours, often classified as 'Internet Use Disorder'.

Furthermore, the blue light emitted by digital screens disrupts our natural sleep patterns, suppressing melatonin production - the hormone responsible for sleep induction. Poor sleep quality, in turn, increases vulnerability to various psychological disorders, including depression and anxiety.

Addressing the mental health effects of digital overload requires an acknowledgment of the problem and subsequent implementation of digital detox strategies, which, coincidentally, are the topics of later chapters of this book.

3.5. Steps Towards Healthier Digital Practices

Awareness of the detrimental impact of digital overload on our brain and cognition is the first step towards healthier practices. Several strategies can be employed to combat digital overload:

1. Setting boundaries on screen time, especially around bedtime.

2. Intentional digital breaks or 'digital sabbaticals'.

3. Disabling unnecessary notifications to limit digital distractions.

4. Engaging in cognitive exercises to strengthen attention and memory.

5. Participating in mindfulness practices to boost focus and reduce digital-induced stress.

In conclusion, our brains are dealing with an unprecedented onslaught of information in this digital epoch. Recognizing the impacts of digital overload is necessary for our cognitive well-being and mental health. However, it's not all grim; armed with understanding, we can take actions to foster a harmonious relationship with technology, turning it into an enhancing tool instead of a depleting one. This ultimately champions a more fulfilling, conscious life, where the digital world becomes an ally to our mental prosperities rather than an antagonist. It is not about demonizing technology but about harnessing it responsibly. For we steer technology, it does not steer us.

Threads of notions discussed in this chapter interweave with themes explored in subsequent chapters, where we delve into how digital overload affects our emotional well-being and relationships, the rising challenges in children's screen use, and the promising solution sector of digital detox.

Chapter 4. Physical Backlashes: The Body's Response to Excessive Screen Time

In the contemporary era, a pervasive digital environment shapes our daily routine, and indulgence in technology continually expands. While we revel in the seamless convenience and connectivity ushered in by the digital age, we inadvertently expose ourselves to a plethora of physical implications arising from excessive screen time. As we grapple with this novel digital struggle, we must underscore the importance of understanding the repercussions of digital overuse on our physiology, and armed with this understanding, navigate the terrain towards a healthier, more balanced relationship with technology.

4.1. The Physiological Impact of Digital Overuse

Excessive screen time reflects not only on our minds but our bodies as well. The increasing prevalence of screen-related health issues such as digital eyestrain, circadian rhythm disruptions, and sedentary lifestyle diseases embody the risk of a digitally dominated existence. Each of these issues unveils a layer of damage as one faces prolonged periods of screen time.

Digital eyestrain or computer vision syndrome incurs a range of ocular discomforts, including blurred vision, dry eyes, headaches, and neck and shoulder pain. These afflictions typically emerge after more than two hours of uninterrupted screen exposure. Severe cases may encounter double vision, red eyes, and polymyalgia. The pixel-based images that digital screens project necessitate sharper focus, and the perpetual adjustment of our eyes to conform to these screen standards more often than not results in visual discomfort.

Excessive screen time also disrupts our circadian rhythms or internal body clocks. Blue light emitted from screens, if viewed late into the night, obstructs the release of the hormone melatonin, which signals our body to prepare for sleep. Consequently, our sleep quality deteriorates, leading to sleep deprivation. Chronic sleep deprivation, in turn, catapults a cycle of health concerns, including a weakened immune system, cardiovascular disease, diabetes, and an increased risk of mental health disorders.

Prolonged sedentary behaviour, a by-product of escalating screen time, exacerbates our physical health risks. Extended periods of sitting can lead to early death, independently of other risk factors such as smoking. Other health hazards might include obesity, hypertension, and heart disease. It can upset the glucose metabolism level, promoting the rise of type 2 diabetes.

4.2. Embracing Proactive Measures for Physical Well-being

This cascade of physical health risks demands a receptive and proactive stance. As we recognize the real and present dangers of excessive screen time on our bodies, we should initiate measures that protect us from these preventable health threats and incorporate habits that promote digital-physical balance into our routines.

To counter digital eyestrain, one might embrace the 20-20-20 rule: every 20 minutes spent using a screen, you should look at something 20 feet away for 20 seconds. Moreover, positioning your screen so that it's not too close to your eyes and minimizing glare from lights and windows can alleviate the strain on your eyes.

To mitigate the impact of blue lights on sleep, consider activating "night mode" or a similar feature on your device that reduces blue light exposure. Consistent sleep schedules and a digital curfew - banning devices in the bedroom at least an hour before sleep - can also bolster your sleep quality.

Sedentary behaviours associated with excessive screen time, signify the importance of incorporating physical activity into our digital lives. Regularly moving and stretching, setting timers to stand and move around every half hour, sticking to a regular exercise routine and walking during phone calls, can subtly intersperse physical activity into daily routines.

4.3. The Road Ahead: Towards a Healthier Relationship with Technology

An indulgent reliance on digital technology paints an alarming portrait: that of rampant physical health issues threatening to compromise our overall well-being. Consequently, acknowledging the potential physical ramifications of digital overuse equips us with the insight to develop a more conscious and informed relationship with our screens. The healthy coexistence with our digital companions hinges upon integrating digital tools into our lives in a balanced manner that prioritizes our physical health.

The journey towards a healthier you in the digital age is about adopting a proactive stance, making intentional choices, and weaving in digital wellbeing habits into our routines. It invites us to shape our environments, rather than be shaped by them, and steer the helm towards a more balanced, healthier lifestyle that doesn't compromise our physical health. Above all, it calls for transforming the digital world from an imposing threat into an empowering tool, capable of enhancing our lives rather than diminishing it. To physically thrive amidst digital excess, we must reclaim our screen time, and usher in a new era of using technology as a bridge to better health, personal growth, and life-enhancement rather than as a barrier.

Even as the digital space continues to evolve and permeate our lives, personal well-being remains paramount. Recognizing the physical toll of unchecked screen time is the first step towards fostering a balanced relationship with technology. It is equally crucial to establish healthy habits, encourage regular check-ins, and continually reaffirm our commitment to living better, both online and off. Thus, with awareness, intentionality, and action, we can shape our relationship with technology to create and maintain a nurturing environment for our physical health.

Chapter 5. Emotional Toll: The Impact on Relationships and Well-being

As we wade deeper into the labyrinth of digital dependency, the adverse effects of excessive technology use on our emotional health and the quality of our relationships become increasingly pronounced. Our devices, despite being incredibly useful, often hold a sinister duality, serving both as a conduit for connection and a source of disconnection, especially when it comes to our interpersonal relationships.

5.1. The Intrusion of Digital Devices in the Relationship Realm

A significant aspect of forming and maintaining healthy relationships, be they familial, romantic, or platonic, is being fully present and in the moment. The conversations, shared experiences, and emotional exchanges all contribute to the emotional richness of our relationships. Yet the continual interruptions by beeps, buzzes, and notifications from our digital devices can easily fracture these precious moments of human bonding, thereby negatively affecting our relationships. The effects can range from relatively minor, such as a friend feeling slighted by your divided attention, to severe, such as a child feeling ignored and emotionally neglected.

Technology has great potential to keep us connected with those far from us, but conversely, it can also create an emotional chasm between people physically close to us. A key piece of this sensibility points to the fact that digital communication, while key in maintaining long-distance relationships, often lacks the nuances of face-to-face communication, such as tone of voice and body language, both of which play a crucial role in understanding and empathizing with each other.

5.2. The Impact of Digital Burnout on Well-being

Our digital world never sleeps, and the pressure to keep up with the constant barrage of emails, social media feeds, work communications and news updates can overwhelm even the most resilient among us and lead to digital burnout. This issue becomes particularly potent in the era of remote work, where the boundaries between personal and professional life blur, pushing people to be 'always on'.

Digital burnout, characterized by symptoms like chronic fatigue, impaired concentration, detachment, cynicism, and lower productivity, can affect every aspect of our life, from our work performance and relationships, to our overall mental well-being. Ultimately, digital burnout can be a symptom of the broader challenge of setting and maintaining personal boundaries in a digital world that acknowledges few.

5.3. The Role of Technology in Fueling Negative Emotions

It's important to acknowledge that every "ping" or "ding" from our gadgets is not merely a sound, but a call for attention. This incessant demand for our focus can lead to increased stress and anxiety levels. At a time when health experts globally are declaring stress as a public health crisis, technology, sans regulation, can throw fuel on the fire.

In addition, excessive use of social media can lead to comparison despair and feelings of inadequacy. A rather ironic consequence, seeing as these platforms were built with the promise of bringing people closer. Over-exposure to carefully curated, often unrealistic, portrayals of others' lives can make us feel disillusioned with our own, leading to feelings of low self-esteem, depression, and overall life dissatisfaction.

5.4. Personal Empowerment via Digital Detox

Reversing the ill-effects of our digital lives doesn't imply demonizing technology, rather it encourages a more mindful and regulated use of it. The concept of a digital detox, a voluntary period of disconnection from digital devices, acts as a powerful tool to regain control over our digital consumption. By consciously disconnecting, we enable ourselves to reconnect with the world around us, observe our feelings without distraction, and cultivate richer, deeper relationships free from the shackles of digital distractions.

Taking control of our digital lives and putting technology in its rightful place can gradually restore the balance lost to the emotional whirlwind of digital excess. By fostering digitally healthy habits, we not only improve our relationships and our emotional well-being, but also cast a vote for the kind of life we want to lead: one where technology serves us, instead of us serving it.

Embracing this emotional recalibration paves the way for a more digitally aware and emotionally prosperous society. As with all matters of health, prevention is better than cure.

In conclusion, while the infinite realms of our digital world offer bountiful opportunities for connection, exploration, and growth, it's crucial to maintain a balance between our digital lives and our emotional well-being. Technology, if used mindfully, can be a facilitator, not a hindrance, to healthy relationships and emotional prosperity, underlining the importance of cultivating a balanced, purposeful, and human-focused approach to technology use.

Chapter 6. Children and Screens: The Rising Digital Native Generation

In today's era, the digital landscape is ever-changing, leaving its profound imprint on contemporary society. Countless transformations have taken place, where one of the most noteworthy changes is the rising digital native generation: children growing up amid innovations and technology, shaping the ways they interact and learn. But what are the implications of this shift? What impact does screen time have on a child's learning capacities and well-being? And, how can we manage this seemingly inevitable reality?

6.1. The Definition of Digital Natives

Digital natives are individuals born or raised during the age of digital technology and, therefore, are comfortable using digital devices and the internet from an early age. This is a term first coined by educator Marc Prensky in 2001, and it's of increasing importance as we delve deeper into the digital age. Today's children are the epitome of digital natives, possessing an intuitive understanding and proficiency with technology that often outmatches that of the preceding generations.

The proliferation of digital technology has fused itself into almost every aspect of our lives, and children are not immune to this. Far from being technology-shy, children are boldly stepping into the technology scene, exploring new alleys of knowledge, interaction, and entertainment. Technology — smartphones, tablets, apps, and online games — is their playground.

6.2. The Effects of Screen Time on Child Development

While it's undeniable that technology has offered unprecedented avenues for growth and learning, too much exposure can have detrimental impacts. Studies consistently demonstrate a correlation between excessive screen time and various developmental issues in children. These range from cognitive, physical, emotional, and social problems, which will be explored in detail in the following sections.

6.2.1. Cognitive Effects

Research shows that excessive screen time can negatively impact a child's cognitive development. Studies link high levels of screen time with delayed language skills, short attention spans, and reduced cognitive abilities. These effects are often because digital platforms present information in quick, easily digestible formats, which may impact children's ability to focus, comprehend complex ideas, or engage in imaginative thinking.

6.2.2. Physical Impacts

Long hours staring at screens can also bring about physical repercussions. Prolonged sedentary behavior can lead to obesity in children by reducing their physical activity levels. Digital dependency can result in decreased outdoor play which might have a considerable impact on a child's natural propensity to explore, experiment, and engage in physical activities. Another growing worry is potential eyesight problems caused by constant exposure to blue light from digital screens.

6.2.3. Emotional and Social Consequences

From a psychological standpoint, excessive screen time can have severe impacts on a child's emotional well-being and social skills. Digital content and social media can shape the emotional development of children, often resulting in feelings of anxiety, depression, and issues with self-esteem. Additionally, children may experience disrupted sleep patterns, which can considerably affect their mood and overall emotional health.

In terms of social skills, reliance on digital devices may curb face-to-face interactions. This could hinder the development of social competences, including the ability to comprehend non-verbal cues, maintain eye contact, and empathize with others.

6.3. Navigating the Digital Landscape: Strategies for Effective Screen Time

It's clear that unchecked screen time can be deleterious to children's well-being. However, in an increasingly digital world, complete disconnection is neither practical nor recommended. Rather than attempts to resist the digital tide, a more viable approach is to set effective screen time strategies that promote positive use while thwarting potential negatives.

6.3.1. Tech-Free Zones and Times

One effective strategy for cutting down unnecessary screen time is the establishment of tech-free zones and times. These could be during meals, bedtime, or in specific places like the dinner table or bedroom. Such provisions help children understand the importance of high-quality offline interactions and ensure that technology usage doesn't interfere with essential activities like sleep or family bonding.

6.3.2. Educate About Media literacy

To help children navigate the vast digital landscape safely, providing age-appropriate educational media is a must. Teaching children to analyze, evaluate, and comprehend digital media critically can shape their screen time into a constructive and mindful activity.

6.3.3. Encourage Active Screen Time

Encourage screen time that actively involves children, either mentally or physically. Activities could extend from educational games that stimulate their cognitive faculties to fitness apps that promote physical exercise.

6.3.4. Screen Time Guidelines

Given the mounting evidence of the impacts of screen time, several health organizations have recommended screen time limits based on the child's age. These should ideally be upheld and monitored, ensuring children are not left unattended with a digital device for prolonged periods.

Balancing digital and physical worlds can indeed be overwhelming. Nevertheless, it's a necessary venture if we are to harness the potential of digital platforms for child development effectively. After all, screen time in itself is not harmful; it's how it is used that determines its impact. Managed correctly, it can serve as an efficient tool for learning and widening horizons, bringing the endless digital world right to a child's fingertips.

To conclude, while the rising digital native generation presents challenges, it also offers countless opportunities. But harnessing these opportunities requires concerted efforts to balance screen time and carefully navigate the digital landscape. With the right strategies, we can guide our children through the digital age, enabling them to reap the benefits of technology without falling victim to its potential pitfalls.

Chapter 7. Digital Detox: The Concept and Its Significance

The sound of a smartphone notification, the flashing of a screen, the compulsion to refresh an email inbox - these have become mundane and steadily incessant facets of our lives. We are deeply entrenched within the sphere of digital devices, with their constancy and impact only intensifying. However, amidst this whirlpool of digital inundation, a silent revolution is simmering. This is the world of 'Digital Detox', a conscious decision to step back from our digital dominance and rediscover life outside the screen. This chapter aims to delve deep and uncover the essence of Digital Detox, its significance in our lives, and why it is more than a mere trend, rather a pivotal element in our digitally fuelled existence.

7.1. What is Digital Detox?

A Digital Detox, as the term suggests, is a period of abstaining from the use of digital or electronic devices. It is essentially a time to disconnect from the screens to reconnect with ourselves, our surroundings, and the people who form an integral part of our lives. Surprisingly, this novel concept negates the very essence of the era we are living in – the digital age. Yet, it is this paradox that underscores the burgeoning need for Digital Detox in our lives.

Not restricted to merely abstaining from technology, Digital Detox encompasses a comprehensive understanding and recognition of the excessive attachment that binds us to our devices. The principal focus is on weaving a healthier, more balanced relationship with technology, thus advocating a life liberated from the compulsive clutches of digital devices.

7.2. The Rising Need for Digital Detox

The advent and rapid proliferation of digital technology has resulted in its unprecedented penetration into every sphere of our lives, affecting not only our daily routines but also our mental and physical health. Pervasiveness of screens, social media obsession, a constant urge to stay updated - these are indicative of an over-reliance on digital technology that hampers our ability to focus, think profoundly, and build deep human connections.

This digital overindulgence has triggered a slew of modern ailments, from digital eye strain and sleep issues to more serious disorders such as anxiety, depression, and Internet Use Disorder (IUD). The potential for damage and the need to curb this spiralling screen usage gives rise to the importance of performing a Digital Detox.

7.3. Embracing Digital Detox - A Counter Movement

Unlike other detox plans that focus primarily on physical wellness, the heart of a Digital Detox lies in its dual objective: addressing both the physical and mental health impacts of digital overload. The aim is to rebuild our relationship with technology and restore a wholesome balance between our digital and non-digital lives.

This in itself makes Digital Detox a counter-movement, an act of rebellion against the constant screen gazing, the incessant scrolling, the relentless obsession with remaining digitally connected. It seeks to reinstate the values of mindful engagement, silent contemplation, and direct interpersonal communication, enshrining the humanly experiences that technology often drowns out.

7.4. Benefits & Impact

The benefits of Digital Detox are multi-fold, far beyond those immediately apparent. From immediate impacts such as reduced eye strain and improved sleep, the benefits seep deeper into enhanced mental clarity, decreased anxiety levels, and improved relationship harmony. The primary aim, however, remains a comprehensive transformation - a shift in our approach towards digital technology, making it a tool for our convenience, not an uncompromising tyrant dictating our decisions and behaviour.

Ultimately, the significance of Digital Detox lies in its ability to centre our lives around a more human, real experience. It presents us with an opportunity to absorb the world without any digital interference, and in doing so, facilitates a profound connection with ourselves and the world around us. It sparks a renewed sense of mindfulness, a deeper understanding of our place in the world, and an enhanced capacity for genuine connection.

In conclusion, Digital Detox is not just a concept. It is an invitation to question and reinvent our relationship with technology. It appears as an oasis in the arid landscape of digital saturation, a beacon guiding us towards a balanced, hearty, and fulfilling existence. As we continue to traverse through the digital age, the significance of Digital Detox will only underscore itself, shaping our experiences and defining our very existence. Let us hope that embrace this constructive habit soon, for our lives are too precious to be consumed by screens.

Chapter 8. Preparation: Laying the Groundwork for Your Digital Detox

Determined individuals who are heading into the realm of digital detox often grapple with these questions: where do we start and how do we prepare? The path towards a successful digital detox starts long before you actually start restricting your use of digital technology; it begins with preparation. This preparation involves understanding your relationship with technology, being aware of your screen time and the habits that contribute to it, strategizing ways of curbing digital dependence, and then gradually implementing them in your daily life.

8.1. An Introspection: Understanding Your Digital Use ==

The first step towards preparing for your digital detox lies in gaining a deep, clear understanding of your relationship with digital technology. Become aware of your own digital habits by analyzing how you spend your time with technology, which devices you use the most, and which digital activities prove the most time-consuming. Not just that, but also scrutinize how these activities affect you. Do they de-stress you or make you anxious? Do they encourage productivity or facilitate procrastination? By mapping out your digital landscape, you lay the foundation of a digital detox program that is tailor-made to your needs and habits.

8.2. Tracking Screen Time: Building Awareness ==

Following introspection, the next essential step in your preparation involves tracking your screen time. Digital tools might often be the culprits behind our excessive screen use, but they can also help us rein it in. Most digital devices come with built-in screen time trackers that break down your usage by app or website. Alternatively, third-party apps such as RescueTime provide deeper analytics into your digital habits. Strategize ways of using these tools to get a firm grip on where your digital time is spent. Knowing is the first step to curtailing, after all.

8.3. Change Brings Challenges: Anticipating Difficulties ==

Much like any significant lifestyle change, your journey to digital detoxification won't be devoid of hurdles. Anticipating these challenges can help you better prepare for them. Long-established digital habits often do not fade away easily and your brain might resist new, non-digital ways of doing things. This resistance might manifest as withdrawal symptoms, decreased focus, restlessness, or sometimes even anxiety. Stay aware of these potential repercussions of detox and mentally prepare yourself to ride out these uncomfortable initial phases.

8.4. Crafting Your Digital Detox Game Plan ==

Once you are aware of your digital habits, it's time to craft a plan to change them. A great strategy is setting achievable goals for your detox. For instance, you could plan to halve your screen time in the first week, then reduce it further in the subsequent weeks. Likewise, commit to replacing digital activities with healthier, more mindful ones. Always ensure that your objectives are achievable and measurable, so you see progress and find motivation to continue.

8.5. The Support System: Involving Loved Ones in Your Detox Journey ==

The involvement of your support system cannot be neglected in your digital detox journey. Communicate your plans for detoxification to your loved ones, so that they understand and respect your intent. They can provide indispensable encouragement and keep you accountable to your digital detox rules. Also, their involvement could also inspire them to embark on their own journeys of balanced tech use.

8.6. Gradual Reduction: Taking Small Steps Towards Detox ==

As with any significant lifestyle change, drastic measures rarely lead to sustainable success. Instead, consider a gradual reduction in screen time. This could be as simple as limiting checking emails to certain times of the day or avoiding screens for an hour before your bedtime. Minor compromises with your screen time can lead to successful major transformations.

8.7. Pre-Detox Break: Taking a Mini Detox Before the Real Deal ==

Taking short breaks from technology, or mini-detoxes, can be a great way to test the waters before you jump in completely. Decide on a short period— a weekend, perhaps— when you will disconnect completely from all your digital devices. This short detox will offer you a peek into what lies ahead and help you identify potential roadblocks that you can proactively address for the longer detox journey.

8.8. Setting Boundaries: Designating Device-free Zones and Times ==

Another pivotal step in preparing for a digital detox is setting boundaries for device usage. This includes setting specific zones in your home where devices are not allowed, as well as certain periods of the day when you do not use technology. These restrictions sculpt an environment conducive to your detox journey, by encouraging more face-to-face interactions and mindful activities.

As painstaking as the effort of unplugging from our digital world may seem at first, its rewards — increased mindfulness, holistic wellness, louder inner voices, more meaningful relationships, and so many more — make the journey utterly worthwhile. With the right intentions, continued determination, and structured preparation, a successful digital detox journey is well within reach. Thus, when it comes to digital detoxification, the operative phrase is indeed: Fail to prepare, prepare to fail!

Chapter 9. Performing a Successful Digital Detox: Strategies and Techniques

Embarking on a journey of digital detoxification entails much more than merely turning off your devices. A successful digital detox is a process that demands patience, planning, and the right set of strategies and techniques. Dive into the process and gain insight into the techniques and methods that can you can use to break free from the clutches of digital addiction.

9.1. Understanding Your Digital Habits

To conduct a successful digital detox, you need first to understand your digital habits. Spend a few days monitoring your gadget usage. Jot down the time you spend on each device and everything you do on it, whether it's work-related or entertainment-oriented. This insight will allow you to see how your devices consume your attention, the websites and apps you frequently use, and whether you truly need as much screen time as you believe. This is a critical first step as it enables you to set measurable, achievable goals for your digital detox.

9.2. Setting Clear Goals

On completion of the digital behavior analysis, turn your attention toward setting clear, precise, and achievable goals. Deciding to 'use less technology' is too vague; we recommend setting goals like 'only two hours of non-essential screen time per day' or 'no devices after 8 p.m.'. By crafting specific goals, you can effectively measure your progress and navigate your detox journey with a clear direction.

9.3. Eliminating Non-Essential Digital Activities

Many of our digital activities, upon close examination, are non-essential. They eat into our time without adding substantial value to our lives. Identify these activities in your digital behavior analysis and aim to eliminate or significantly reduce them. This can include endless social media scrolling, excessive news consumption, or binge-watching series. If an activity doesn't provide you with genuine joy, learning, or connection, it most likely falls into the non-essential category.

9.4. Utilizing Tools and Apps

Contradictory as it may seem, certain digital tools can aid us in using technology less. Tools such as website blockers, screen time tracking apps, and push notification silencers can aid in minimizing distractions and limiting time-sucking digital activities. Use these tools to your benefit during your digital detox journey.

9.5. Incorporating Offline Activities

A crucial element in performing a successful detox is incorporating offline activities. By swapping digital activities for their analogue counterparts, you can experience the joy of physical engagement and the richness of real-world interaction. Cook a meal instead of ordering food online, read a physical book setting aside the e-books, engage in a sport instead of a video game, have face-to-face conversations rather than texting. This strategy will help you feel more present, engaged, and fulfilled.

9.6. Adjusting Your Environment

One excellent technique to support your detox journey is by adjusting your environment. Make it conducive to minimal device usage. Keep chargers out of sight to limit the temptation to continually recharge devices. Create designated no-technology zones such as the bedroom or dining area. The key is to set up your space in a way that naturally discourages excessive gadget usage.

9.7. Gradual Detox Approach

For some, going 'cold turkey' with technology can cause more harm than good. If you find your digital habits deeply ingrained, consider a more gradual approach. Begin by setting one tech-free hour each day, and then gradually increase the length of these periods; this approach can also help avoid the possible stress that sudden disconnection might cause while still working towards the same end goal – mindful, balanced use of technology.

9.8. Accountability and Support

You're not alone on this journey. Reach out to a friend or family member and ask them to be your accountability partner. Let them in on your goals and your reasons for doing a detox and request them to check in on your progress regularly. You could even invite them to join you on this journey. Having a support system can make the process far more manageable and enjoyable.

9.9. Taking a Holistic Approach

Finally, remember to be kind to yourself. Slipping up doesn't mean failure, and a successful detox doesn't mean completely eliminating technology. It's about creating a healthier relationship between you and your devices. Each small step towards mindful tech use is a victory in itself.

These strategies and techniques, when incorporated effectively, can guide you smoothly through the process of a successful digital detox. Take note of these, adjust them as per your needs, and embark on a path that will lead you to a more balanced, present, and fulfilling life in the digital era.

Chapter 10. Post-Detox: Maintaining Mindful Use of Technology

After the liberating journey of a digital detox, you have seen firsthand what life can be like when not obsessed with the screen. One might even have relished the slowness of time, the tranquil interaction with the natural world and possibly, the pleasure of indulging in a book without distracted peeks at the mobile. It is though essential to remember that a detox is not an end; rather, it lays the groundwork for a more mindful engagement with technology.

10.1. Continuing the Momentum

Starting to use technology post-detox is not a return to former habits, but a reformed approach towards digital tools. The changes may feel excruciating initially, but the goal is a sustained transformation and not a mere temporal respite from screen enslavement.

First and foremost, acknowledge that technology is not the enemy but our relationship with it requires amending. Technology being a boon can't be overstated, from fostering global connections to simplifying mundane tasks, it helps us in innumerable ways. It's our uncontrolled and mindless usage, not the technology itself, that is cause for concern.

10.2. Cultivating Consciousness

To maintain the gains from your digital detox, practicing conscious usage of technology is an absolute necessity. Be present in your digital interactions and be deliberate about why, when, and how you're using a device. Before reaching out for your device, pause for a moment. Ask yourself why. Is it as an information source for a crucial work project, or could it just be an unconscious habit, a response to boredom or avoidance of uncomfortable feelings? The goal, after all, is to use technology with intentionality and awareness, becoming masters of our devices rather than slaves to them.

Another important aspect of mindfulness involves regularly reflecting on your relationship with technology. Make it a practice to periodically evaluate the time, energy, and other resources that you spend on your devices. Hereby, changes that need to be made, if any, are realized and accomplished effectively.

10.3. Embracing Tech-Free Zones and Times

Establish tech-free zones in your house and designate tech-free times in your day. These keep both spatial and temporal boundaries in your relationship with digital devices, ensuring that technology does not intrude upon every facet of your life. Consider making meal times and the bedroom tech-free. Not only it will promote better sleep hygiene, but it will also enhance the quality of your mealtimes, encouraging connection with others.

10.4. Leveraging Digital Wellbeing Tools

You can also use technology to fight the complications of technology overuse. Most smart devices come equipped with digital wellbeing tools nowadays, such as screen time monitor, app limits, downtime, and others that help you regulate and control your usage. By keeping light on your digital habits, you can identify if this relationship is veering off course and take amendatory actions in time.

10.5. Communicating Your New Digital Habits

It's equally beneficial to communicate with your peer group, local community, or your professional circle about your new digital habits and policies. Not only is this an accountability tool, but it also helps generate greater awareness among others about digital wellbeing. Maybe you will end up helping a friend or colleague to reconsider their relationship with technology!

In conclusion, the post-detox phase, while challenging, represents nothing short of your new life, a more aware, more present one. It's a period to cultivate a healthy relationship with technology that ensures the digital tools serve their purpose as aids in our life, not as means that distract, overwhelm, and exhaust us. With a conscious and intentional approach to technology usage post-detox, you will be better positioned to leverage the benefits of digitalization whilst not falling prey to its potential perils. Maintaining mindful use of technology is a journey, not a definitive destination, and it's this journey that will unfold a richer, more balanced life that integrates the best of the digital and physical world.

Chapter 11. Building a Digital-Physical Balance: The Route to a More Present Life

Building a balance between our digital and physical lives is not just desirable but crucial in today's society marked by digital overreach. As we traverse this critical path towards creating a more present life, we'll learn how to incorporate healthy boundaries, redefine our relationship with technology and build robust habits that nurture our well-being.

11.1. Understanding the Need for Balance

Firstly, it is vital to acknowledge the need for achieving a balance between digital and physical aspects of life. The ramifications of excessive screen time have not only been noticed in our mental and physical health but also in how we relate to other individuals and the world around us. It's no longer an isolated phenomenon, but rather a complex issue that straddles work-life, personal relationships, and self-development. While technology facilitates our day-to-day tasks, its overuse can lead to isolation from our surroundings, poor health, and weakened interpersonal bonds. Thus, dedicating time to both digital and physical pursuits is key in leading a well-rounded life.

11.2. Setting Boundaries with Technology

Our march towards building a digital-physical balance begins with setting boundaries. Boundaries breed respect - respect for our time, our needs, and our values. This means consciously defining where and when we will use our digital tools and sticking to these rules. For instance, keeping gadgets out of the bedroom to nurture superior sleep, setting aside certain hours for offline activities, or allocating specific times for checking emails and social media updates. These boundaries ward off unwarranted interruptions and make us more intentional with our tech use.

11.3. Conscious Tech Consumption

One of the pivotal methods towards achieving a balance is conscious tech consumption. This implies being mindful and selective about the digital content we consume, ensuring that it enriches our lives and fosters growth. Whether it is tuning into a podcast that widens our perspectives, devouring e-books that fuel our knowledge, or leveraging apps that augment productivity, conscious tech consumption is about choosing quality over quantity.

11.4. Fostering Digital-Free Zones and Times

Creating digital-free zones and times serves as havens of tranquillity in our bustling lives. These spaces or periods, devoid of digital intrusions, allow us to disconnect and immerse ourselves in the sounds, sensations, and the beauty of the present moment. Whether it's devoting the first hour after waking up to some quiet contemplation, establishing tech-free dinner times for quality family interactions, or declaring certain areas in the home like the bedroom as gadget-free zones, these intentional spaces pave the way for nourishing experiences that reconnect us with the physical world.

11.5. Embracing Tech-Free Activities

Nurturing offline hobbies and pursuits are great counterbalances to our digital lives. Whether it's exploring the outdoors, playing a musical instrument, painting, reading a physical book, or engaging in community work, such activities keep us grounded while enhancing our skill set, unleashing our creativity, and offering profound satisfaction.

11.6. Regular Digital Detox

Regular digital detox sessions, with intervals that work best for you, could reap significant benefits. These sessions present opportunities to reassess our digital habits, find space for introspection, and rekindle our relationship with ourselves and the world around us.

11.7. Adopting Mindful Technology Use

Mindful technology use can be a powerful tool to maintain the balance between the digital and physical. This involves paying full attention to our actions while using technology, observing how much time we spend, how we feel during and after the use, and pondering whether it adds value or simply robs us of our precious time.

11.8. Building Resilience

Finally, building resilience is a key aspect of maintaining a digital-physical balance. We're bound to falter on this journey. We might overuse technology, fail in our digital detox attempts, or get drawn in by the allure of the digital world. However, each stumble is an opportunity to learn, adjust, and improve.

In conclusion, the journey to building digital-physical balance isn't about vilifying technology; it's more about optimising it to enhance our lives. It's about fostering a healthier, conscious relationship with technology, which respects our need for personal connection, solitude, and the pleasure of the physical world. By adopting these methods, we can hold control over technology, rather than being at the mercy of it, leading to a more balanced, present, and fulfilled life.